Original title:
Under the Shade of Monstera

Copyright © 2025 Creative Arts Management OÜ
All rights reserved.

Author: Micah Sterling
ISBN HARDBACK: 978-1-80581-787-1
ISBN PAPERBACK: 978-1-80581-314-9
ISBN EBOOK: 978-1-80581-787-1

## **Wrapped in Nature's Arms**

In the jungle where plants like to play,
A leaf whispered secrets of the day.
I tripped on a root that thought it was cool,
The vines giggled loudly, calling me a fool.

Frogs wore tiny hats, ready for a ball,
While ants strutted by, feeling ten feet tall.
The sun peeked through, just to be the boss,
And threw a party, but I was the loss.

A parrot cracked jokes, he was quite the star,
While bugs formed a band with a ketchup jar.
I tried to join in, but got stuck in a vine,
And laughed so hard, I'd forgotten my line.

So here I am, tangled up in the fun,
Nature's got humor, second to none.
With leafy companions, I can't help but smile,
In this wild green world, I'll stay for a while.

## Embrace of the Jungle Spirit

In the wild where shadows creep,
Lounge with plants that never sleep.
Laughter blooms like sunny rays,
Dancing vines in leafy plays.

Sipping drinks from strange coconuts,
Bamboo straws that make us strut.
Monkeys swing and join the fun,
Chasing dreams beneath the sun.

## Sanctuary Amongst Giant Leaves

Hiding from the buzzing bees,
Whispering secrets to the trees.
Costumed bugs in funny hats,
Throwing parties, even with cats!

A lizard slides on leafy paths,
Snickering at the world's laughs.
We sip tea with jungle friends,
Joking about where the wild ends.

## Serenity Beneath Verdant Veils

Sipping smoothies, what a treat,
Fruits and laughter, oh so sweet!
A parrot jokes, a sloth nods slow,
Time has no rush, just a gentle flow.

Bouncing ferns in breezy plays,
While the sun through leaves just rays.
In this realm, all worries fade,
Life's a game, and joy is made.

## A Shelter of Fronds

Pillow of leaves, cozy and soft,
A home where tropic creatures loft.
Squirrels in capes, ready to jest,
Join our gathering, be our guest.

Dancing ants with tiny shoes,
Host a ball with wild views.
In the embrace of green delight,
We laugh and sing into the night.

## Lush Green Hideaway

In the jungle of my room,
Plants gossip in their bloom.
They plot to steal my snack,
The sneaky leaves never lack.

When friends come over to play,
They stumble, fall, and sway.
I laugh as they collide,
With vines that choose to hide.

Every corner has a guest,
A fern that's quite the pest.
In this jungle, I reign,
Amongst creatures so insane.

## Whispers in the Foliage

The leaves, they share a tale,
Of a snail who called for mail.
They chuckle at his plight,
While I sip my juice at night.

The shadows dance around,
As I hear a silly sound.
A lizard serenades my shoe,
Bouncing like it's on a zoo!

In this world where plants converse,
I ponder if I'm in verse.
But laughter fills the air,
Even when I shake my hair.

## Secrets of the Leafy Canopy

Among the stems, a secret lies,
An ant who dreams of the skies.
He wishes on a leaf for wings,
To join in on the birds' swing.

The shadows play a game of peek,
With sunlight making them squeak.
While I attempt my yoga pose,
A cheeky pot plant gently doze.

Oh, the drama in green thickets,
Where tiny voices weave their tickets.
I laugh till my sides are sore,
In this leafy jungle lore.

## Dancing Shadows on Tile

On the tiles, shadows prance,
As plants hold their goofy dance.
I try to keep my balance neat,
While they wiggle with their beat.

There's a bug who thinks he's slick,
Doing cartwheels, oh so quick!
He bumps into a flower's face,
And they both end up in a race.

In this space where laughter flows,
Nature hosts its silly shows.
Who needs a TV screen,
When foliage reigns as queen?

## Beneath the Whispering Greens

In a jungle of leaves, I go to hide,
Where petals giggle and branches glide.
The sun peeks in, but the plants just grin,
They know my secrets, let the fun begin!

A squirrel winks, as it steals my snack,
While vines tickle toes, with no hint of lack.
The air is thick with laughter and play,
Here in the greenery, I'd love to stay!

## **Solace in a Leafy Retreat**

A shady spot where the lizards dance,
In this green haven, I take a chance.
The breeze whispers jokes in rustling leaves,
While critters conspire, oh how it deceives!

A butterfly slips on its own silly feet,
Wobbling awkwardly—oh, what a treat!
The foliage tickles, it brings me to tears,
In this cozy nook, I'll forget my fears!

## The Enchanted Leafy Dome

Inside a canopy that protects my head,
Where vines joke around, never feeling dread.
The sunlight giggles as it sneaks on through,
What a charming light show, oh, how it grew!

A frog croaks loudly, claiming it's a star,
While worms tell stories from near and far.
In these leafy halls, where whimsy thrives,
I find my joy, where laughter arrives!

## A Tapestry of Shadows and Light

A patchwork of shadows, a giggle parade,
The light plays tricks—oh, what a charade!
Every rustle a riddle, every whisper a game,
Who knew nature's humor could spark such acclaim?

An ant in a suit, seeks dramatic flair,
While bees buzz by without a single care.
In this garden of laughter, the world feels right,
I'll stay with the greens, and bask in the light!

## Tales from the Leafy Embrace

In a jungle where the vines tickle feet,
Laughter weaves through the air, oh so sweet.
Bugs tango on leaves with leaky pajamas,
Nature's dance, sans drama, it's all just a charmer.

Squirrels perform acrobatics on high,
While the parrot cracks jokes as it flies by.
The air is rich with giggles and glee,
As frogs play the banjo, jazzing the spree.

## Echoes of Green in Quiet Corners

In the nooks where the shadows start to grow,
Whispers of mischief playfully flow.
The ferns gossip about the sneaky breeze,
While ants hold a meeting, plotting with ease.

Caterpillars strut, they think they can fly,
In their mind's eye, they're kings of the sky.
But when they fall flat on their tiny behinds,
The laughter erupts, oh, nature's designs!

## **The Curl of Nature's Embrace**

Curling leaves wrap secrets tight,
Where the sun chuckles, gleaming bright.
Goblins of green play hide and seek,
In a world of wonder, they can't be meek.

Rabbits in bow ties sip on dew,
Debating broccoli – is it green or blue?
The wisdom of plants, a catchy pursuit,
They throw leafy parties with snacks that loop.

## Dreams in the Tropical Hush

As shadows stretch, the night takes a peek,
Fireflies blink in a waltz, oh so cheek.
The moon leans in, with a grin on its face,
Dreams swirl and twist in a leafy embrace.

A raccoon in shades runs a midnight show,
With jokes so cheesy, they steal the glow.
Beneath the stars, no worries, no fuss,
Just laughs in the night, as nature whispers plus.

## Foliage Fantasia

In the jungle of my dreams, I find,
A plant with a grin that seems quite unkind.
Its leaves wave hello with a quirky flair,
I try to escape, but it's just not fair.

Lurking behind, with a rogueish glee,
It tickles my nose, oh what could it be?
A monster or friend? I can't really tell,
But as I sneeze loudly, it laughs oh so well.

## Calm in the Chaos

Life's a whirl, yet here I rest,
Among leafy giants, I feel quite blessed.
They rustle and giggle at my silly plight,
As I sip my drink and bask in the light.

One leaf curls up for a sneaky peek,
It whispered, 'Hey buddy, don't you dare squeak.'
The chaos outside starts to blur and bend,
With a snicker, I think, what a marvelous friend!

## The Canopy Beneath the Stars

Looking up at the green, I see a sight,
Leaves dancing wildly, oh what a delight!
Stars peek through gaps, timid and shy,
As I watch the plants ponder, oh my oh my.

A lizard slinks by, in a top hat he came,
He tipped it to me and got caught in a game.
The leaves burst with laughter, their joy so profound,
It's a circus tonight, in this leafy playground!

## Green Horizons

On a lazy afternoon, the sun shines bright,
I find a patch of green, oh what pure delight.
The leaves start to wiggle, they mischievously sway,
I ask them for secrets, but they choose to play.

In this tranquil garden, I chuckle and grin,
As the vines come to life, ready to spin.
With each little quirk, they tickle my fate,
In the garden of laughs, I'm never too late.

## **Under Layered Green**

In a jungle of leaves, I find my way,
My friends are plants, they never stray.
I dance with the vines, we giggle and twist,
In this leafy world, nothing's amiss.

Sipping dewdrops, it's quite a feast,
I munch on sunlight, say the least.
With chlorophyll dreams, we paint the air,
Who knew plant life could be so rare?

## A Symphony of Shadows

The shadows are quaking, they're feeling bold,
Telling tales of secrets, adventures untold.
A leaf above whispers, 'Come play with me,'
I nod with a laugh, it sets my mind free.

With every rustle, a giggle escapes,
Beneath the green cover, we plot silly shapes.
We wrestle the branches in a leaf-filled brawl,
Laughter erupts, echoing through the hall.

## Leafy Lullabies

In the quiet of green, lullabies play,
The leaves sing soft songs at the end of the day.
A cocoon of laughter, we sway to the beat,
With every soft rustle, we're dancing on heat.

Among the bright hues, I take a strange nap,
Waking to find I'm wrapped in a gap.
"Is this a jungle gym?" I start to declare,
The leaves just giggle, they don't have a care.

## Flourishing Whispers

Whispers of green, they chatter and tease,
Sharing their gossip, as I catch the breeze.
A tropical riddle, wrapped up in a leaf,
With puns about sunlight, they spark joy, not grief.

They poke fun at the squirrels, skittering about,
"Look at those furs, they make such a clout!"
I join their laughter, though I'm a bit shy,
Who knew leafy chats could make time fly?

## **The Hidden Oasis**

In a jungle of socks, I lay in bliss,
Unruly plants turn my home to a quiz.
Where's the remote? It must be a breach,
Among leaves and shadows, they teach me to preach.

Cousin Gary claims he feeds it too much,
But it's thriving, I say, with every green touch.
The leaf monster grins; it gets all the light,
While my houseplants conspire to start a plant fight.

## Boughs of Tranquility

A leaf fell down, didn't make a sound,
Dodging my cat, always looking profound.
Is this a plant or a housemate friend?
With its whiskers of fronds, it won't ever bend.

In the corner lurks my leafy roommate,
Deciding our dinner on a flexible plate.
I swear it's plotting to grow arms and legs,
While I prepare salad with avocado pegs.

## Under the Verdant Sky

The sun creeps in, takes a peek at my stash,
Dancing with shadows, making quite the splash.
A party of leaves with a doorman of vines,
Hiding my snacks, oh, the treachery shines!

My neighbors just smile, they're used to the scene,
A bungalow jungle, quite the greenery sheen.
No more space for shoes, it's all leafed out,
Sipping on tea, what's this all about?

## **Life in the Leafy Abode**

Trapped in a web of green, spritely and spry,
Could it be sentient? I just might comply.
It mocks my routine, down to the last crumb,
For it knows all the secrets—the ultimate sum!

A dance-off ensues with the potted crew,
Each twist and turn says, 'What will you do?'
They sway with delight, while I sip my brew,
As we share my home, oh, what a hullabaloo!

## Beneath the Verdant Canopy

In the jungle's playful clasp,
Lizards dance and snakes all gasp.
A parrot drops a fruity snack,
And all the critters come to snack.

Chillin' with a vibrant crew,
Sipping nectar, oh so blue.
A monkey swings with one wild leap,
While down below, I start to creep.

Giggling leaves with jokes to tell,
What's the true height of a shell?
Does it make sense, this lizard's grin?
Or is it just the sun's warm spin?

With shadows playing peek-a-boo,
I wonder what the ants will do.
With every rustle, laughter grows,
In this green world, joy overflows.

## **Roots and Dreams Intertwined**

Tangled roots beneath my feet,
Is there coffee here to meet?
I stumble on a gnarled knot,
And wonder why I tied the knot!

A squirrel's stash of acorns bright,
Confused, they scatter in delight.
"Hey, that's mine!" the other shouts,
As the frenzied chase breaks out.

Dreams are sprouting, wild and free,
Like seedlings in a jolly spree.
What if they dance in a conga line?
Or join the birds for a chat over wine?

So here I sit, a curious guest,
While nature plays, I take my rest.
I'll join the roots in this ramble,
And share a laugh, a little gamble.

## Life Amongst the Lush Greenery


Life erupts with silly sights,
Where bugs do silly bug-like flights.
A snail complained, "This leaf's too high!"
While frogs croak jokes, oh what a guy!

Vines swing like they've lost their mind,
Entwined in laughter, so unconfined.
A chameleon dreams of striking blue,
But blends instead in the morning dew.

Dancing shadows, a leafy cheer,
As breezes tickle without fear.
A chipmunk's wiggle steals the show,
While plants gossip, "Did you see that glow?"

What fun it is, this world alive,
Where even roots can learn to thrive.
In every twist and leafy swathe,
There's laughter sprouting, undenied faith.

## **Mysteries in the Leaf's Pattern**

What secrets lie within each vein?
Is it a map or a train of grain?
"Hold on tight!" the leaf did shout,
"Adventure's near, without a doubt."

Patterns twist like jester's flips,
The sun joins in, it's quite the trip.
A beetle joins, he rolls his ball,
"Let's make a game, we'll have a ball!"

"Wanna bet in shades of green?"
A leaf critter said, with a gleam to glean.
Who knew foliage had such flair,
With whispers soft as a summer air?

So join this dance, the leafy show,
Where laughter blooms and breezes blow.
With every flutter, joy aligns,
In this wild realm, good fortune shines.

## The World Beneath Broad Leaves

In a jungle gym of green,
Where shadows dance and laugh,
A squirrel tells a pun,
While a snail takes a photograph.

Laughter echoes in the breeze,
As ants break into song,
They juggle tiny acorns,
Claiming nature can't go wrong.

A frog leaps with a grin,
On a lily pad so wide,
He croaks a joke so funny,
Even fish can't hide.

Beneath these vast, broad leaves,
The world's a playful stage,
With nature's critters laughing,
Turning every leaf a page.

## **Nature's Green Veil**

Behind curtains of bright green,
Lies a world that likes to play,
A parrot tells a riddle,
While the wind sweeps it away.

The bees buzz in a chorus,
As they waltz from bloom to bloom,
They gossip 'bout the flowers,
In a fragrant little room.

A raccoon raids the pantry,
With a mask and full of glee,
Finding snacks beneath the leaves,
Who knew nature loved to spree?

Nature's veil is full of fun,
With tomfoolery and cheer,
Join the merry little dance,
And laugh without a fear!

## Secrets in the Shade

In a dappled, leafy nook,
A wise old owl gives advice,
But he can't stop his own giggles,
When the bats start playing dice.

A hedgehog spins a tale,
Of thorns that weren't so prickly,
While the butterflies laugh quietly,
Oh, how they flutter sickly!

The shadows swish and sway,
With grasshoppers on a spree,
They plan a daring picnic,
But it's not quite bug-free.

Secrets dwell in funny places,
Where whimsy loves to hide,
Among the secrets leafy vast,
Is laughter as our guide.

## Where Light Meets Leaf

When sunlight kisses green,
And shadows start to sway,
A lizard performs stand-up,
In a comical display.

The crickets chirp their laughter,
As they tap-dance a duet,
While the bumblebees take selfies,
With flowers, fancy-set.

In this laughter-laden grove,
The secrets shyly play,
While the funny little critters,
Bring another sunny day.

Where light and leaves collide,
The joy is wild and free,
So come and join the revelry,
Beneath the boughs of glee!

## **Embracing Nature's Canvas**

In the jungle gym of green,
Lizards race, quite a scene.
Sipping juice from a fresh coconut,
While the monkeys laugh, they strut!

A snail debates its slow, slow pace,
While ants plan a wild chase.
Bugs breakdance on a leaf,
Nature's jesters, beyond belief!

Frogs croak jokes, what a delight,
With fireflies joining the night.
A toucan cracks a corny pun,
Life's a show, oh what fun!

So grab a chair and take a seat,
Nature's laughter, oh so sweet!
In this leafy, vibrant space,
Every moment's a silly race!

## **Beneath the Leafy Canopy**

Beneath leaves as big as umbrellas,
Squirrels wear tiny propellers.
A bird sings out a crazy tune,
While I giggle at a raccoon's cartoon!

Butterflies dance with flair so bold,
Somewhat stoic, but never cold.
Grasshoppers hop, they twist and twirl,
Creating chaos in a little swirl!

Caterpillars write haikus on trees,
While bees buzz round with utmost glee.
Nature's humor, oh, such a blast,
These moments of mirth, they surely last!

In this leafy world, we play and roam,
Finding laughter as we call it home.
Unleash your joy, let worries stray,
For here, the funny reigns today!

## Whispering Green

The leaves around whisper quite funny,
With secrets that gleam like honey.
A chameleon plays peekaboo,
Winking at me, 'I see you!'

Two snails argue who's super fast,
While the ferns giggle and wave, amassed.
In a thicket, a vine's got sass,
It tickles me, a green morass!

Birds tease squirrels about their fluff,
Saying, 'That tail's just way too tough!'
Nature's comedians in grand display,
Making us smile through the day!

In this enchanted, leafy scene,
Laughter echoes, truly serene.
Nature's quirks are never far,
In this green realm, we're all a star!

## Enchanted by Foliage

Once a tree thought it could dance,
But fell over, missed its chance!
Flowers giggled at the sight,
As the squirrel chased its tail in fright!

Dancing shadows, what a show,
The groundhogs cheer, 'Go, go, go!'
Ladybugs in tuxedos roam,
Clipping tickets as they comb!

The vines twist tales of bumpy rides,
Whispers shared on gentle tides.
A caterpillar, dressed in style,
Flaunts his stripes with a broad smile!

In the kingdom of emerald leaves,
Nature spins laughter like magic weaves.
Each chuckle dances on the breeze,
Join the fun, let laughter please!

## Natural Reflections

In green whispers, shadows play,
A lizard struts in a silly way.
He thinks he's suave, a true charmer,
But he's just a bug's alarm-er.

The fern giggles, sways in delight,
As sunlight dances, oh what a sight!
While ants march by in a stylish line,
A parade of tiny, critter design.

A squirrel glares, with nuts in hand,
Planning mischief, oh so grand.
He climbs the trunk with epic flair,
Only to find, it's a leafy snare.

Through chattering roots, laughs do rinse,
Nature's oddities make no sense.
Each moment's strange, a quirky plot,
Keep laughing life, so don't be caught!

## Beneath Verdant Giants

A raccoon prances with a hat so wide,
The leaves chuckle, oh what a ride!
He thinks he's slick in the leafy stage,
But hurries away—nothing's his wage.

A butterfly winks, in colors bright,
Losing his charm in his fanciful flight.
He flutters past, oh what a tease,
While ants march on with exacting ease.

A toad croaks out a joke or two,
But what he says? No one has a clue!
The shadows giggle, oh so sly,
As he awaits his buggy pie.

With sun above and leaves below,
Nature's antics steal the show.
In this jungle of green delight,
Laughter grows, beneath the light.

## The Heartbeat of the Leaves

In the rustle of leaves, a secret's told,
A squirrel's gathering treasures, so bold.
He stashes nuts like a hoarding king,
 Unaware of the bird's endless zing.

A worm sings softly, a squishy tune,
His dance is funky, beneath the moon.
Leaves sway along in a leafy shuffle,
 Nature's rhythm in glorious huddle.

A caterpillar winks, 'I'll fly someday!'
But for now, he munches in a leafy buffet.
With every bite, his dreams expand,
'Till wings emerge, and he's in demand.

The shade is alive, laughter resounds,
Through the canopy, joy knows no bounds.
With every breeze and small delight,
Life's heartbeat leaps, oh what a sight!

## Canopies and Care

In the morning light, a spider spins,
Webs of laughter, where mischief begins.
A breeze comes by with a cheeky nudge,
Leaves whisper secrets, and trees won't judge.

A funny bird with a beak quite long,
Tries to sing but gets it all wrong.
His tunes fall flat, like a pancake flop,
But in nature's eyes, he's still top shop.

A gopher pops up, with a dirt-filled hat,
Winks at the sun, then dives with a splat.
He giggles loudly, a carefree chap,
In this leafy dwelling, there's no mishap.

Amongst the green, delight is rare,
Laughter lingers, filling the air.
In every corner, joy takes its stake,
Under the green, life's sweetest wake.

## The Calm Amidst Foliage

In corners green, I hide and peek,
A chatty bug speaks, it's quite the cheek.
With leaves like hands, they wave and sway,
Inviting mischief to frolic and play.

A squirrel with style, in spandex he prances,
While worms plot their dance in careless trances.
The sun breaks through, a spotlight it gives,
To these leafy antics, my heart truly lives.

Chirps from the branches, a comedy show,
As nature giggles, it steals the glow.
I sip my drink, a tropical splurge,
While fauna perform, it's all quite a surge.

With every rustle, a new joke appears,
Tickling my thoughts and easing my fears.
In laughter's embrace, the world feels so grand,
Surrounded by humor, I take a stand.

## Shelter in the Leaves

A canopy high, with whispers so bold,
Where laughter and jest turn the usual cold.
Frogs wear tiny hats, it's quite the sight,
While ants march a parade, from left to right.

Beneath the broad curls, a picnic ensues,
Where fruit flies float in a party of hues.
A rather rude crow steals my last slice,
But the laughter of crickets makes it all nice.

Nearby, a gopher makes a grand show,
Standing up tall, like a pro in a row.
He tumbles and rolls, oh what a delight,
While I can't help but chuckle at his flight.

A breeze whispers secrets of funny things spry,
As shadows befriend me, they dance and lie.
In this lush retreat, my cares drift away,
With humor and joy, I've found my new play.

## where Shadows Flourish

In dappled light, where shadows do twirl,
Lurking mischief starts to unfurl.
A lizard with swagger, he struts with glee,
While snails race at speeds only they could decree.

Amidst the green, they trade silly tales,
Of echoing giggles and wind-swept fails.
The breeze is a rascal, tickling my nose,
While squirrels debate in their puffy fur clothes.

Fungi sport hats, bringing flair to the floor,
While caterpillars moan, then dance through the door.
In shadows that flourish, the laughter is grand,
As nature invites me to join in the band.

So I cozy in close to a leafy domain,
While the parodies play, life's simple and plain.
With every quick giggle, my spirit takes flight,
In this thriving embrace, everything feels right.

## **Nature's Soft Embrace**

In this plush retreat, my laughter ignites,
The flora's bright charm, makes everything light.
A parakeet prances, with flair on a vine,
While worms share their secrets on sipping moonshine.

Leaves wiggle in rhythm, with jokes from the breeze,
As I peer at the antics of bees in the trees.
A wise old owl snoozes, then suddenly winks,
While ants make a racket as everyone thinks.

From laughter to jests, the chorus resounds,
Echoing through greens, where humor abounds.
Playing hide and seek, shadows join in the fun,
While whispers of joy dance 'til day is done.

So here in the lush, I find my delight,
With nature's soft giggles, life feels just right.
As the sun dips low, and stars come alive,
In this tapestry woven, I happily thrive.

## The Language of Leaves

When leaves start to chat, it's a riot,
They gossip and giggle, never quiet.
Dip in a dip, a twist in a spritz,
Plants make great pals, they're wittier than wits.

A fern talks of fashion, a palm tells a tale,
Each one claiming glory, every plan to unveil.
"Leaf me alone!" cries a shy little bud,
While succulents blush in their cozy green mud.

## Sanctuary of Serenity

In a leafy retreat where fun never ends,
The vines swing like monkeys, you'll find no pretends.
Dancing shadows play peek-a-boo with the light,
While the air is alive with pure plant delight.

A cactus gives high-fives, with prickles in tow,
While daisies debate where the best breezes blow.
"Stay here with us!" the orchids all plead,
In this shady haven, all worries are freed.

## Evoking the Tropics

A parrot cracks jokes with a bright sunny squawk,
While lizards loom large on their favorite rock.
Coconuts chuckle as they roll down the lane,
In this vibrant space, there's never a pain.

Bananas wear bonnets, all yellow and bright,
Laughing together as day turns to night.
With every leaf rustling, there's mischief and cheer,
Tropical vibes say, "Come join us, my dear!"

## Forest of Dreams

In a forest of dreams where the silly plants grow,
The trees share tall tales and the breezes blow slow.
Mushrooms in costumes dance under the blue,
While fireflies flash secrets, just for a few.

A sloth gives a wink, with a grin ear to ear,
As the crickets play tunes that you just want to hear.
"Rest not in haste!" sings the wind through the leaves,
In this whimsical realm, joy is what we achieve.

## The Playlist of Plant Life

When the leafy friends all gather,
A dance-off breaks the mundane chatter.
Rhythms of breezes, they twirl and sway,
Singing to sunlight, come join the fray!

Cacti spin with prickly grace,
Add some groove to that dry place.
Ferns do the cha-cha, wild and free,
Even the succulents join in glee!

Vines climb high, a funky beat,
Petals flounce, can't stand still, they cheat!
Nature's jiving in green attire,
Come join the party, feel the fire!

At dusk they chat, no one feels shy,
"Do you think we touch the sky?"
Rooted in fun, that's a plant's rave,
The playlist of life, oh the shenanigans we pave!

## Swaying in Serenity

In the quiet grove where leaves do dance,
A gentle breeze gives plants a chance.
To rustle softly, to giggle low,
As nature's rhythm puts on a show.

Laughter echoes through the green,
Even petals play, light and keen.
A gnome up high says, "Look at me!"
While daisies snicker, feeling free.

Moss carpets hide some giggly toes,
As dandelions plot the next big shows.
"Who's the fairest?" asks a shy fern,
"Oh, it's definitely you!" they all discern!

In leafy lounges, they sip sunlight,
Chasing shadows till the night is bright.
So let it be known, in this calm retreat,
Nature's jokes are silly, yet sweet!

## Nature's Warm Embrace

In the corner of the cozy nook,
Plants whisper secrets in their book.
With tendrils curled, they share a tale,
Of how they won the veggie trail!

Look at the ferns with their frilly swish,
In unison, they make a wish.
"Let's play hide and seek!" the ivy cried,
While the daisies giggled, trying to hide.

The sun beams down, a golden ray,
As blooms wear crowns, they dance and sway.
"Ever felt the warmth of sunburned cheeks?"
Said the leaf to the petal, "We're unique!"

With nature's arms wrapped all around,
Life is silly, laughter's profound.
Together they bask in the blissful haze,
A humorous warmth in leafy displays!

## Patterns of Sunlight

Sunlight dapples, a playful tease,
Painting shadows with leafy ease.
"Look at my stripes!" a leaf calls out,
While others giggle, without a doubt.

The rhythm of light, a jigsaw scene,
Patterns of colors where plants convene.
"Shall we play tag?" a branch suggests,
While petals twirl in their lovely vests.

Oh, to bask in the golden glow,
To dance with leaves in a lively show!
Nature's artistry blooms with cheer,
Where even the weeds crack a grin here.

Filtered beams, a vibrant game,
Each twist and turn, never the same.
In the joyful light, let's all engage,
As we laugh and play on nature's stage!

## Shelter in the Tropical Oasis

In the jungle, play hide and seek,
With little green friends, oh so unique.
They peek and giggle, giving us glares,
"Is that a human?!" Oh, what a scare!

We sip on smoothies, all green and lush,
While lizards dance, their tails in a rush.
The sun spills in, a bright golden glare,
But here in the leaf fort, we haven't a care!

## Melodies of the Canopied World.

A choir of birds on a swing, they chirp,
In a leafy hall where laughter can blur.
Their songs are silly, with no real tune,
Dancing beneath the bright silver moon.

With vines like ropes, we climb to the top,
To see the whole world, in a colorful mop.
But watch out now, a monkey might swing,
And drop his bananas! Oh, what fun they bring!

## **Green Canopy Dreams**

In the green labyrinth, I stumble and roll,
Mossy shoes squeak, losing all control.
Chasing butterflies that taunt and tease,
Dodging raindrops like floppy frisbees!

We hide from the sun, in shadows we sprawl,
Where whispers of leaves laugh, "Let's play ball!"
Frogs jump and ribbit a tune so absurd,
Every hop sounds like a laughter heard.

## **Leaves Whisper Secrets**

The leaves gossip softly in the cool breeze,
"Did you hear what the coconut said with ease?"
They chuckle and rustle, a leafy affair,
As critters join in and swing from the air.

A turtle strolls with a hat made of fern,
"Fashion icon!" the parrots all learn.
Boys in the grass play tag with the sun,
While the big fruit bats just laugh and have fun!

## Celestial Greens

In a jungle so bright, plants wear their hats,
The leaves do a jig, while squirrels chat.
Sunlight sips tea in a leafy tea house,
While frogs play piano, all quiet as a mouse.

Laughter echoes through roots like old vines,
A bird in a tutu shows off its designs.
The snails move like dancers, all slow and grand,
Belting out tunes, a slimy band.

## Tales of the Canopy

A raccoon in pajamas raids the snack stash,
While butterflies gossip, their colors splash.
Caterpillars wear glasses, they think they're so wise,
Debating the best way to eat fruit pies.

Lemurs on stilts stir up a dance,
While a hedgehog tries to join in their prance.
But rolling away, he skids out of sight,
The crowd roars with laughter at his little plight.

## A Garden of Take Flight

Fluffy clouds tickle the tops of the trees,
While hummingbirds dance on the whims of the breeze.
A lizard in sunglasses sips lemonade,
As roses tell jokes, never to fade.

The breeze lifts the whispers of flowers unfurled,
As marigolds tease, saying, 'Look at our world!'
Votes go to daisies for the best quip,
And daisies retort, 'We make all the trips!'

## Embracing Earth's Palette

Colorful gossip spills from each leaf,
As daisies discuss their latest motif.
Twirling around, the ferns share their style,
While mushrooms giggle, it's all worth the while.

A chubby raccoon in a bright polka-dot,
Thinks he's a model—oh, isn't he hot?
The worms roll their eyes, and they start a slow cheer,
'You're a fashion icon, let's make that clear!'

## **Vegetal Reverie**

In a jungle of leaves, we sip our drink,
Giggles echo, what do plants think?
A cactus wears a sombrero, it's true,
While ivy whispers, 'Hey, howdy-do?'

Snakes pretend to be jump ropes in vain,
Ferns throw parties, can you blame them?
Lettuce joins in, with a dance so spry,
Celery shimmies under the sunny sky.

Chill out with the orchids, so laid back,
With every chuckle, the world feels less whack.
We play peek-a-boo with the dandelion,
Laughing like kids, just pure joy, divine!

So raise a glass to the leaves so grand,
In this leafy place, we'll always stand.
Nature's humor always makes me grin,
Around every turn, good times begin!

## **Treetops and Tranquility**

Look up high, what do you see?
A squirrel in shades, just as cool as me!
Branches wave like they're telling a joke,
While birds drop beats—oh, how they croak!

The laughter rings as chipmunks parade,
In a conga line through the sun's cascade.
Each leaf is a smile, each stem a laugh,
Nature's comedy is our favorite craft.

Moss acts shy, nestled on the ground,
Telling tall tales without making a sound.
In this breeze, even calm folks can cheer,
With playful spirits, there's nothing to fear!

So join the fiesta in branches up high,
Swing with the wind, let your worries fly.
With joy all around, don't let it fade,
In this whimsical world, let laughter cascade!

## Hidden Worlds in the Green

Behind every leaf, there's a little plot,
Where fungi wear hats, and snails connect dots.
Ladybugs gossip, sharing the news,
While tulips bloom in their vibrant hues.

A rabbit rehearses his stand-up routine,
As butterflies giggle, 'Oh, that's so keen!'
In the shadows, plants throw wild soirees,
With radical roots getting lost in a haze.

A patch of grass takes a selfie today,
With daisies posing, enjoying the sway.
Nature's own studio, laughter's the key,
Where every bloom dances so wild and free.

So if you wander through lush, bright scenes,
You'll find laughter grows thick in the greens.
Join in the ruckus, let joy take its flight,
In hidden worlds, life is pure delight!

## Below the Foliage

Under the leaves, the laughter's loud,
Caterpillars groove in a hefty crowd.
A tulip throws shade, it's quite the scene,
While a grasshopper jumps in a fit of glee!

In the shade of ferns, they tell party tales,
As dandy lions discuss their sales.
Every petal's a comedian in bloom,
Spreading joy in the afternoon gloom.

Oh, the snacks here are always first-rate,
A feast of pollen that birds celebrate.
So gather around, let the fun begin,
In this leafy hangout, every laugh's a win!

So crack your best jokes, let your spirits rise,
Through the dappled light, let hilarity fly.
In this green world, where the fun doesn't cease,
Let laughter grow loud, and your worries decrease!

## Lush Serenity

In a jungle where plants gossip,
Lively vines twist and flop,
Greenery flirts with the breeze,
As I trip over my flip-flops.

Ferns wave like they know me,
Whispers float on the air,
Cacti roll their prickly eyes,
As if they just don't care.

A palm tree's shade is my throne,
Monkeys swing with flair and style,
I sip on my iced coconut,
And laugh at the world for a while.

The soil's a mess, what a sight,
Worms wiggling, joining the fun,
In this riot of leafy delight,
Who cares about getting things done?

## Tropical Embrace

With gigantic fans waving high,
My plants act like little clowns,
They dance in the tropical sun,
While I just lounge around.

The sunflowers stand up tall,
But the monsteras just slouch,
It's a circus out in my yard,
Who knew plants could be such a grouch?

Leprechauns forgot their gold,
But found shade in my patch,
They joke about rainy days,
And all I do is catch.

Succulents share silly tales,
Of their adventures in drought,
While tropical ferns roll their eyes,
I'm just here laughing it out.

## Shadows of Growth

In the midst of tangled leaves,
A squirrel throws a wild party,
Nuts fly like confetti,
And I'm the reluctant hearty.

Others walk their fancy dogs,
While I walk my leafy crew,
They laugh as vines tie me up,
It's quite an odd zoo.

The shadows stretch and yawn,
As the sun dips just right,
Plants giggle at the ants,
Probably cause of their height.

What chaos in cozy gloom,
As I sip on herbal tea,
Each leaf greets me with a wink,
In this quirky jubilee.

## **A Dance of Foliage**

Tonight's the leaf disco night,
With fronds swaying to the beat,
A cactus spins in its pot,
While a fern taps its feet.

Banana leaves shimmy and swirl,
Like they're auditioning for fame,
While I shuffle on my way,
Trying to dodge the plant blame.

The philodendrons jive along,
With fans waving, all in cheer,
Each clash of branches and stems,
Makes the neighbors twitch in fear.

So here's to the wild parade,
Where greens do their goofy dance,
In this party of plant delight,
I found joy in every glance.

## Conversations with the Botanical

I asked a leaf what it has seen,
It giggled softly, oh so green.
"I've witnessed gossip from the breeze,
And heard the whispers of busy bees!"

The soil chimed in, with dirt and pride,
"I hold the secrets where dreams reside!
I'm not just muck, I'm history grand,
I cradle roots that wiggle and stand!"

A pot perched high had things to say,
"I'm more than decor, hear my bouquet!
With every bloom, a joke I tell,
About the plants that grow so well!"

At dusk we laughed, a leafy crew,
With petals and stems, a jubilant view.
In this botanical chat, pure delight,
Who knew green could shine so bright?

## Calming the Wild Heart

The cactus sighed in quiet glee,
"Prickly? Yes, but I'm carefree!"
It cracked a joke about a near miss,
A squirrel's slip that ended in bliss!

Beside it, ferns danced with flair,
"We sway in joy, without a care!
While people rush and rarely pause,
We sip on sunshine, what a cause!"

Oh, how the roses snickered in bloom,
"We steal the spotlight, banish the gloom!
With fragrant jokes and petal pun,
We turn the day from work to fun!"

And there I sat, with a heart so light,
In the company of greens, there's no fright.
Laughter bursts where wild things start,
Life's amusing tones calm the wild heart.

## Nature's Embrace in Urban Life

A rubber plant shared a tale so bold,
"I'm a city dweller, if truth be told!
On rooftops high, we chill all day,
Making concrete jungles feel like a café!"

The ivy climbed walls with style and grace,
"I'm the wannabe superhero of this space!
I scale heights in my leafy attire,
While folk below just tire and tire!"

A succulent winked bright in the sun,
"I take my time, with water, that's fun!
When everyone rushes, I just relax,
Sipping sweet droplets, with no need for hacks!"

In this urban jungle, we plant our tale,
With laughter and joy in every gale.
Amidst the chaos, we grow and thrive,
Nature's charm keeps the city alive!

## Shadow Play on the Ground Below

Beneath broad leaves, shadows played,
A dance of light that never strayed.
"I'm just a shadow, don't make a fuss,
But here, my friend, we can discuss!"

The sunlight giggled, casting bright,
"From dawn till dusk, I've seen the light!
While shadows prance with attitude,
I beam with joy, not a hint of feud!"

A falling leaf drifted with grace,
"Oh, I'm the champion of this place!
Watch me twirl, it's all in fun,
Leaves and shadows dance, never done!"

So let's rejoice in the playful scene,
With laughter echoing, evergreen.
In the warm embrace of the day's soft glow,
Let humor bloom where the shadows go!

## Life in the Lush


In the thick of green, I stumble around,
My hat's on sideways; I'm lost, not found.
A coconut falls with a thud on my foot,
I laugh as I wave, pretending I'm cute.

Lush leaves are dancing, a silent conga,
They wiggle and jive, saying, 'Hey, come along!'
A squirrel in a suit, oh what a sight,
He adjusts his tie, ready for flight.

Beneath the big fronds, I trip on a vine,
This jungle's my stage—my mishaps divine!
With every misstep, I chuckle and sway,
Who knew being clumsy could brighten my day?

So here in the greenery, laughter is king,
Life's a fun circus, join in for the fling!
With bugs as my audience, I strike my best pose,
In this vibrant setting, each day's a new rose!

## Shadowed Serenity

With shade from the leaves, I sip my mint tea,
Listening to whispers, oh, what could they be?
The ferns gossip softly about the sun's plans,
While I just smile, holding crumbs in my hands.

A gecko with glasses reads poetry loud,
While a squirrel in shorts gathers nuts from the crowd.
I nod in agreement, their wisdom is real,
In this world of shadows, I'm learning the deal.

A breeze carries laughter as I catch my breath,
Laying on grass, I flirt with sweet death.
A bee buzzes by, attempting to sway,
But I'm too busy laughing at the game the leaves play.

In this leafy haven, where fun rules the day,
True joy is found in a quirky ballet.
With sunbeams and giggles, I twirl and I spin,
Among shadows and laughter, I delight in this grin!

## A Haven of Green

In a jungle of laughter, I trip on a root,
A monkey just chuckled, 'How cute, how cute!'
My summer hat's floppy, my ice cream's all gone,
But the cheeky palm fronds are waving me on.

With plants on my left and the bugs on my right,
I'm caught in a dance, oh what a delight!
There's a sloth doing yoga, a snail on a quest,
Who takes such small steps like it's all just a jest.

The vines weave their tales of jungle romance,
While I join the critters in this silly dance.
Tickled by tickles, I laugh at the scene,
In the depths of the green, life's a carnival dream.

So let's sway with the branches, don't be such a bore,
Embrace the weirdness; it's life's greatest score!
With joy echoing loud, the colors will blend,
In this haven of green, let the fun never end!

## **Embracing Nature's Reflections**

In the mirror of leaves, my hair's a wild mess,
A frog wears a crown—new king of the quest!
I giggle and twirl, as the sun's rays prance,
With shadows of plants, I engage in a dance.

A parrot talks gossip, I can't help but stare,
It likes to tell secrets without a care.
A caterpillar whispers, with plans drawn so grand,
'One day I'll be flying; fly high, understand?'

Elbow-deep in blooms, I roll with delight,
While bugs pull their pranks under soft fading light.
The trees serve me cocktails in glasses of dew,
In this charming escapade, anything's true!

Beneath the green cover, where laughter ignites,
My heart's light as air, this bliss feels so right.
With sunshine above and silliness near,
In reflections of nature, I banish all fear!

**Tranquil Hues**

In a leaf's embrace, I seek my fate,
Laughter blooms and worries wait.
The plant's wide grin, a leafy friend,
Shakes off stress like it's a trend.

Beneath the green, my thoughts take flight,
Whispers of joy, a leafy delight.
Chasing shadows, the sun takes a peek,
Nature's joke—it's never bleak.

Each sip of air, a comic tease,
Tickling senses, like a gentle breeze.
A leafy lounge where giggles thrive,
In this green space, I feel alive.

So come and sit, let laughter bloom,
In the heart of green, there's always room.
With leaves as laughter, and roots so deep,
Join the fun, dive in, don't peep!

## **Oasis of Calm**

A leafy throne where I recline,
Jokes spill out like vintage wine.
Plants don hats, they share their cheer,
Under this canopy, there's no fear.

Twirling vines in a leafy dance,
Nature's circus, come take a chance!
Laughter echoes through the fronds,
Creating stories that respond.

Who knew that leaves could start a joke?
With every rustle, the silence broke.
In this haven where light does play,
Cactus costumes lead the way!

Smiling greens in a playful plot,
Finding humor in every spot.
In this oasis, fun is the norm,
Join the laughter, it's always warm!

## In Nature's Grasp

Grassy pranks with roots aglow,
A banquet of chuckles, come join the show.
Leaves gossip softly, what do they know?
Antics unfold like a lively tableau.

In the grasp of green, mischief reigns,
Tails wag as the sunlight wanes.
A playful breeze kicks up some fun,
Turning moments into everyone's run.

Twinkling lights through branches hide,
Whispers of nature, a cozy guide.
Every rustle hints at a jest,
Where smiles blossom, that's truly the best!

So gather 'round, let's share a laugh,
Nature's punchline is always daft!
In this embrace, let joy adhere,
Life's funny dance, we hold it dear!

## Canopy of Comfort

Beneath the green, where giggles grow,
A canopy where silly winds blow.
Weathered jokes and canned delight,
Under the leafy, whimsical light.

Each tendril twists like a prankster's smile,
Nature's spirit goes the extra mile.
Breezy banter without a care,
Let's find comfort in this playful air.

From the branches, chortles descend,
Leafy letters from a ferny friend.
Together we chuckle through sunshine and shade,
In this cozy space, there's no charade.

Unfurling laughter, soft as the breeze,
In this green paradise, we laugh with ease.
So take a seat, don't be aloof,
Nature's comedy—time to goof!

## **The Hidden Poetry of Leaves**

In the jungle of green, with leaves so wide,
Lies the secret laughter, where shadows glide.
A monster of nature, with style so sleek,
Whispers of humor, in every peak.

Sipping the sunlight, while flaunting their flair,
These leaves conspire, with jokes in the air.
They tickle the breeze, as they twist and twine,
Who knew such foliage could be so divine?

With a wink from a leaf, I giggle then pout,
Who knew a plant could bring such a shout?
They dance in the breeze, doing leafy ballet,
Just foliage here, having a play-day!

Hidden in shadows, where the laughter grows,
Each leaf a smile, in nature's prose.
So let's gather 'round, for a chuckle or two,
In the leafy embrace, where giggles breakthrough.

## Resting in Foliage's Grasp

In the shade of green, where giggles abound,
Laughter echoes softly, without a sound.
A cozy cocoon, with leaves as the quilt,
Snug as a bug, where joy is built.

With leafy companions, I settle down low,
Trading my worries for a funny show.
A rustle above, like a whispering glee,
'What's green and giggles? It's us, wait and see!'

Grappling with branches, I trip and I slide,
The leaves start to chuckle; they're my leafy guide.
Together we frolic, with humor in tow,
In foliage's grasp, all worries forgo.

Cradled in laughter, as shadows persist,
Just a goofball plant, oh how could I resist?
We share a chuckle, as sunshine peeks through,
Strutting in green, making memories anew.

## Breath of the Monstera's Heart

Beneath the broad leaves, where whispers conspire,
Lies the heart of humor, that never will tire.
Jokes hidden in veins, like secrets kept tight,
The breath of this plant is pure comedic delight.

With each playful breeze, the leaves giggle out loud,
Spilling their jokes, like a raucous crowd.
Who knew foliage could have such a wit,
As nature's own stand-up, we're all here to sit!

Swinging like vines, oh what a display,
The plants throw a party, they know how to play.
So lock up your worries, let laughter take flight,
In the heartbeat of greenery, everything's bright.

So breathe in deep, let the humor unfold,
The heart of the monster is a sight to behold.
Each leaf a comedian, in this green sanctuary,
Where laughter is plenty, and worry's a rarity.

## In the Company of Giants

Surrounded by giants, in leafy attire,
They tower above me, like dreams to inspire.
With gusto they wiggle, and sway in the light,
Making me chuckle; oh what a sight!

These colossal companions, with leaves oh-so-large,
Lead me on adventures, they're in charge.
With roots in the ground and stories to tell,
In this leafy realm, we giggle and dwell.

'What do you call plants that dance and jest?'
The giants snicker quietly, 'Leaves at their best!'
I join in the laughter, as shadows grow long,
In their leafy embrace, I find where I belong.

So here we gather, in foliage so grand,
Sharing our tales, hand in leafy hand.
With every new joke, the giants declare,
In the company of greens, life's a humorous affair!

www.ingramcontent.com/pod-product-compliance
Lightning Source LLC
Chambersburg PA
CBHW070315120526
44590CB00017B/2690